BEAKMAN'S WORLD

A Visit to the Hit TV Show

A Visit to the Hit TV Show

Based on the Newspaper Feature
"You Can with Beakman and Jax"
Created by Jok Church and
Distributed by Universal Press Syndicate

A TVbooks, Inc. Production

Andrews and McMeel
A Universal Press Syndicate Company
Kansas City

Library of Congress Cataloging-in-Publication Data

Beakman's world: a visit to the hit TV show / based on the character by Jok Church ; [produced by TVbooks, inc. ; edited by Ed Wyatt].
p. cm.
"A TVbooks, inc. production."
Summary: The star of the television program "Beakman's World" answers questions, presents amazing facts, and performs experiments on a variety of scientific topics.

ISBN: 0-8362-7005-3 $8.95
1. Science – Study and teaching – Audio--visual aids – Juvenile literature. 2. Television in education – Juvenile literature. 3. Beakman's world (Television program) – Juvenile literature. [1. Science. 2. Beakman's world (Television program) 3. Television programs.] I. Church, Jok. II. Wyatt, Ed. III. TVbooks, inc.
Q196.B4   1993
500 – dc20   93-20637
            CIP
            AC

Produced for Andrews and McMeel by:
TVbooks, Inc.
8513 SE 68th Street
Mercer Island, Washington 98040

Edited by Ed Wyatt
Additional writing: Rick Dujmov
Book layout and design: Jeff Hostetter
Production coordinator: Tom T. Crouch
Video screen captures: Lance Kyed, Desktop Post, Inc.

CONTRIBUTORS
From the TV Show "Beakman's World"

Writers:	Episodes One Through Six: Jok Church, Stephanie Phillips, Phil Walsh, Barry Friedman, Dan DiStefano, and Mark Waxman
	Episodes Seven and Eight: Richard Albrecht, Casey Keller, Phil Walsh, Barry Friedman, Dan DiStefano, and Mark Waxman
Chief Researcher/ Segment Producer:	M.J. Miller
Science Consultant:	Al Guenther
Photo Credits:	John Rinker and Carin Baer

Actors:
  Beakman: Paul Zaloom
  Josie: Alanna Ubachi
  Lester the Rat: Mark Ritts
  Penguins: Alan Barzman and Bert Berdis

Table of Contents

How is a pie like a volcano? See page 19.

Who is this famous dead guy? See page 30.

What do lobsters and dreams have in common?
See page 49.

How do leaves change color in the fall?
See page 57.

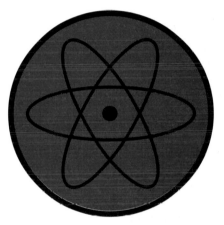

What is the element Beakmanium (Bk)?
See page 81.

Can sound travel through cheese? See page 87.

"Hi! My name's Beakman... and you've just broken into Beakman's World!"

So here I am on my monumental mission to describe how the world works...to illuminate upon the mysteries of the universe...to explain life in terms you've never heard before...to describe complex principles in terms you'll now understand. That's what we do on "Beakman's World," and that's what we do in this book. If you want to know what we don't do, just listen to what my friend here has to say.

Prof. I.M. Boring
Inert State University

Hello. My name is Professor I.M. Boring. I prefer a different method of learning about science and the world around us. I believe we should read large books with very small writing and no pictures. I believe we should learn by digesting facts and repeating them over and over again. I also believe in showing film strips that go "beep" when it's time to switch the picture, but it never works out, and the whole film strip gets out of sequence so the voice is talking about nuclear fission and you're looking at a picture of a three-toed sloth. That's the traditional method of learning science, which I like to refer to as "The Boring Method."

"See what I mean! Now that's some scary stuff."

Well, it's time to do what I do with the people who help me do what I do. I love what I do and I do what I love. But what I love to do is whatever I can do for you.

Name: Josie

Position: Lab Assistant

Personal Characteristics:
Curious, inquisitive, bright,
intelligent, smart,
energetic, patient.

Job Description:

- Act as Beakman's sounding board.
- Organize Beakman and his world.
- Coordinate all questions submitted to Beakman's World.
- Assist Beakman in various hands-on lab experiments and demonstrations.

Name: Lester

Position: Disgruntled Actor in Rat Suit

Personal Characteristics: Know-it-all, skeptical, unfluffy.

Job Description:

- Assist Beakman and Josie with lab experiments.
- Provide criticism and skepticism to any or all (mostly all) of Beakman's demonstrations.
- Make the sublime ridiculous.
- Try to look good in the rat suit.

Rain, Beakmania & Volcanoes

"I realize that all of us kind of look alike, but I'm Herb...you're Don."

"Do you remember what our life was like before Beakman, Don?"

Chapter

Rain

"Where do puddles go after it rains?"

Well, to show you that, I'll need to make a puddle. I'll take a bowl and put in a pinch of precipitation and a dash of dirt. Now, if we add sunlight in the form of a beautiful Scandinavian plastic lamp, we'll be able to demonstrate where the puddle goes after it rains.

Eventually after it rains, the sun comes out and beams its rays down on the puddle.

As the heat of the sun warms up the water in the puddle, the water EVAPORATES, which means it turns into an invisible gas called WATER VAPOR. The water vapor then rises up into the sky. As it rises, it cools. The higher up you go, the colder it gets.

When the water vapor gets cold, it CONDENSES, which means it squeezes real tightly together and the vapors turn back into tiny little drops of water. The drops bunch up and form clouds. When the tiny drops grow too large to be held in the clouds, they fall as raindrops. Then the sun comes out, the water evaporates, and the whole process begins all over again. This is called the WATER CYCLE.

You can see how the water cycle works by looking at your clothes dryer. As the wet clothes are warmed by the dryer, the water evaporates and forms water vapor. The water vapor comes out through the dryer vent. You can't see it, because it's invisible, but if you held a really cold can of soda in the water vapor, drops of water would form on the can. This is CONDENSATION, like what happens to the water vapor from a puddle as it rises high in the sky and cools off.

Volcanoes

"What's the deal with volcanoes anyway?"

"Anyway?"

"Anyway."

If the earth were the size of an apple, the part of it which we humans have explored would only be as thick as the apple's skin. The reason we don't know much about the inside of the Earth is because the Earth is just too doggone difficult to drill through.

Anyway, like earthquakes, volcanoes are among the most powerful forces in nature.

The top layer of the Earth, which averages about 20 miles thick, is called the CRUST. The next section is called the MANTLE, and it's about 1,800 miles thick. In the lower crust and upper mantle are pockets of hot melted rock called MAGMA.

"So, what's lava?"

Because of all the heat and gases in magma, pressure builds up and forces the magma out of a weak section in the Earth's crust. It oozes out gently or explodes out violently. Either way, it's called an ERUPTION.

LAVA is what magma is called after it comes out of the volcano.

Another way to think of a volcano is to think of a pie. The pie's crust is like the Earth's crust. And the filling inside the pie is like the hot rock far below the surface of the Earth. And the steam you see escaping from the crust is like the gases from a volcano. But, of course, a pie doesn't explode like a volcano...

"I challenge you to get the Queen of Hearts to make the water stay in a glass of water when you turn it over."

You're gonna need:

- two glasses of water
- a Joker
- the Queen of Hearts

Warning

"Experiments should be performed at home only with adult supervision and all appropriate safety precautions should be followed exactly and no sub-stitutions should be used. And...do this experiment over a sink!"

First, we'll try it with the Joker. Fill the glass with water. Put the Joker on top. Then, turn the glass over. What happens? The Joker cannot make the water stay in the glass.

Now, let's get down to business. Take another glass of water. Place the Queen of Hearts on top of the glass, and hold it there as you turn the glass over. Then, slowly take your hands off the card. Behold...the card stays in place, and the water stays in the glass!

See, there's something all around us called AIR PRESSURE. And even though you can't see it, we live at the bottom of an ocean of air, and all that air pushes on us. The air around the card actually pushes up against the card harder than the water in the glass pushes down on it.

In fact, you'd need a glass of water over thirty feet high before the water would weigh enough to push the card off the glass!

BEAKMANIA

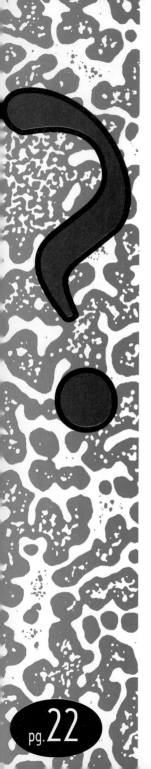

"And now, the one you've been waiting for! The quarterback of questions...the King Kong of knowledge...the Duke of discovery...the Elvis of experimentation...the B-man himself! Ladies and gentlemen, we give you the one...the only...the Beakman!"

Q: What is one of the world's most remarkable fishes?

A: One of my favorites is a fish called the Plaice. The plaice disguises itself from other underseas enemies by changing the colors and patterns on its body to match its surroundings. In fact, the plaice is so incredibly good at this, that it can match the pattern of a checkerboard!

Q: Dear Beakman, what animal lays the biggest egg?

A: The ostrich, the largest bird on earth. Out of a single ostrich egg, you could make an omelet large enough to feed twelve people!

Q: Hey, Beakman, how many hamburgers can you get out of a cow?

A: It depends on how nicely you ask. Actually, out of one cow, you can get about 400 quarter-pounders.

Q: What's the biggest volcano on Earth?

A: The biggest volcano is Mauna Loa on the island of Hawaii.

Q: How much ice is there in Antarctica?

A: There is so much ice in Antarctica that if it would ever all melt, the level of the world's seas would rise about 200 feet on Earth, and a quarter of the dry land would be submerged.

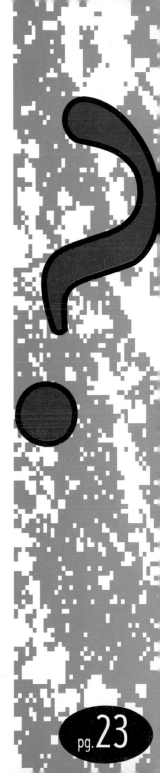

Gravity, Beakmania & Inertia

"Hey, it's a chapter on gravity."

"Finally, we'll understand the mysteries of Beakman's hair!"

Chapter

FACT!

Bees kill more people each year than sharks.

pg. 26

Gravity

"If the Earth is round, why don't the people on the bottom fall off?"

Gravity is the invisible force that pulls things towards the Earth's center. Without it, we'd have a hard time staying put. In fact, we'd be put out...into space! We can try to overcome gravity, but we can't turn it off.

"How about other planets? Is it true that there's no gravity on Jupiter?"

Actually, there's no night life there. But seriously folks, Jupiter has lots of gravity. There's much more gravity on Jupiter than down here on Earth.

Well, this is a tricky question. First of all, there is no bottom to the Earth, really. It may look like it. I mean, you can point to the bottom of a globe, but globes are just models. If you look at the Earth from space, there is no up and down and no top or bottom. It all depends on the way you look at it. But even if there were a bottom of the Earth, we couldn't fall off because of GRAVITY...it's the law!

In fact, you would weigh two-and-a-half more times on Jupiter than on Earth. The reason is that Jupiter is the largest planet in our solar system. You see, the more MASS ("stuff") that something has, the stronger the gravitational pull. And because Jupiter is so massive (So large that 1,000 Earths would fit inside it), the pull of gravity on its surface is more than twice what it is on Earth.

Inertia

"Why do I have to wear a seat belt?"

lives a year? The reason why has to do with something called INERTIA.

The man who "discovered" inertia was Sir Isaac Newton (see page 30). Newton came up with three laws of motion. The first one says, "If something isn't moving, it won't start moving until something makes it start moving."

An excellent question! Did you know that seat belts were first patented in 1903, but didn't become standard in all automobiles until 1968? And that if everybody wore their seat belts, it would save up to 13,000

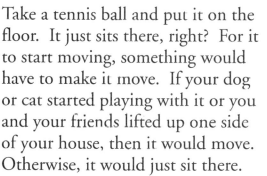

Take a tennis ball and put it on the floor. It just sits there, right? For it to start moving, something would have to make it move. If your dog or cat started playing with it or you and your friends lifted up one side of your house, then it would move. Otherwise, it would just sit there.

Now the second part of the law goes something like this: "If something is moving, it won't stop moving until something makes it stop."

When you're in a moving car, it will only stop if you apply the brakes, or if you happen to run into something, like a telephone pole or a wall. And, that's why you should wear a seatbelt... because when you're in a car and it stops, you keep going! Unless your seatbelt is there to hold you in your seat.

Finally, the third law says, "To every action there is an equal and opposite reaction." Sir Isaac Newton will demonstrate how this law works on the next page.

Famous Person

Name: Sir Isaac Newton
Born: 1642.
Died: 1727.

Claim to fame: Supposedly was hit on the head by an apple, thus prompting the discovery of gravity.

Famous quote: "To every action there is an equal and opposite reaction."

Favorite cookie: Fig Newton

Although the apple on the head story is most likely made up, Newton's discovery of gravity is incredibly important. In addition, Newton also developed the Three Laws of Motion:

1st Law: If something isn't moving, it won't start moving until something makes it start moving.
2nd Law: If something is moving, it won't stop moving until something makes it stop.
3rd Law: To every action there is an equal and opposite reaction.

In the top picture, you can see that everything is at rest. Then, the broom handle strikes the cardboard...the cardboard makes the paper tubes move...but the eggs are held in place by their inertia. Good old gravity, however, pulls the eggs down into the glasses.

COOL FACTS ABOUT THE PLANETS

Mercury: Mercury is like somebody who hangs out by the pool all summer. It's basically a mass of rock and iron that spends its time baking in the sun.

Venus: It's kinda hot and windy on Venus. Forecast: about 891 degrees Fahrenheit, with winds in the neighborhood of 217 miles per hour.

Mars: Mars is the only other object in space besides our Moon that has visible surface features when you look through a telescope. Scientists have yet to find little green men living on Mars.

Jupiter: It's the biggest planet. Despite its size, Jupiter is just a giant sphere of gases.

Saturn: Famous for its rings, Saturn has 18 moons and has a surface temperature in the neighborhood of minus 279 degrees Fahrenheit. That's pretty darn cold.

Uranus: Uranus is a "tipped" planet, with its axis tilted at a 98 degree angle. As a result, each pole experiences 42 years of light, then 42 years of darkness. Talk about a long winter.

Neptune: The "blue" planet has a storm system called "The Great Dark Spot," that is the size of the Earth. That's one storm you don't want to get caught outside in.

Pluto: The most recently discovered planet (1929), Pluto is made up of mostly water ice (strawberry or grape), with a crust of methane.

BEAKMANIA

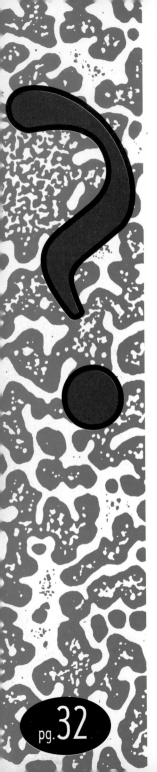

"Get ready! It's time to mash your mind! Here he is, the regent of replies...the nabob of know how...the one...the only...the Beakman!"

Q: What sport has the fastest-moving ball?

A: In the game of jai-alai (pronounced "high'-lie"), the ball can travel up to 188 miles per hour. In comparison, a baseball pitched by Nolan Ryan can travel at around 100 mph.

Q: Hey, Beakman, how much does a hummingbird weigh?

A: Most hummingbirds weigh less than a penny.

Q: Why do hummingbirds hum?

A: Because they forgot the words...actually, the humming is the sound their wings make as they flap seventy times a second.

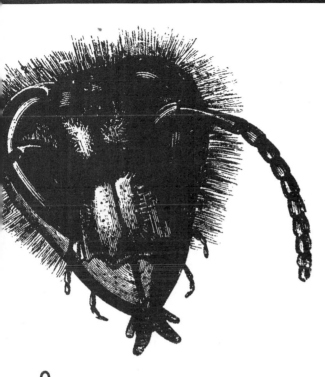

Q: How much nectar from flowers do bees need to make a honeycomb?

A: Good question. In order to make a one-pound honeycomb, bees must collect the nectar of more than two million flowers.

Q: That's amazing. Got any other quick facts?

A: How about this? The blue whale doesn't have to eat for about six months. It can survive by feeding off its own blubber.

Q: What was the first word spoken on the moon?

A: Okay.

Q: I said, what was the first word spoken on the moon?

A: Okay.

Q: What was the word?!!

A: "Okay" was the first word spoken on the moon. Buzz Aldrin, the astronaut, said it from the spacecraft when it landed. All right?

Okay.

Noises, Beakmania & Snot

"I'm afraid there's some really disgusting stuff in this chapter."

"Too bad, now hurry up and turn the page, I can hardly wait."

Chapter

Noises

"What's all that scary creaking and cracking I hear when I'm trying to sleep at night?"

Well, it's not monsters, because monsters aren't real. But the noises you hear <u>are</u> real. They're caused by your house and your furniture changing sizes.

"Come on, Beakman, give me a break."

Really, they are. The reason your house and furniture change sizes at night is that it's cooler at night. When things get cool, they get smaller. This is called CONTRACTION.

Let me give you an example. If you were to take an inflated balloon and put it in a freezer, when you pull it out later, it will be smaller in size. Taking the same balloon and placing it in the hot sunlight will increase its size.

This happens because the balloon is made of MOLECULES. A molecule is the smallest amount of something you can have. They are everywhere...the balloon is made of molecules, the air inside the balloon is made of molecules, and even you (yes, you) are made of molecules.

When the molecules of air inside the balloon are cooled, they slow down. And when they slow down, they don't need a lot of room to zip around.

So the air inside the balloon contracts, and so does the balloon. Now, when you heat up the balloon, the molecules are excited, and speed up. They need more room to zoom, so the balloon has to expand. This is called, naturally, EXPANSION.

The same thing happens to your house. At night when things cool off, it contracts. During the day, when things are warmer, your house expands. The noises you hear at night are most likely the wooden joints rubbing together in walls, windows, and doorways.

Snot

"Say, Beakman... um...what is...snot?"

Excellent question! Some might think it's a gross question, but this is Beakman's World! Any question goes. We're here to tell the truth about life itself. "Snot" is slang or what we call a colloquialism for the scientific term MUCUS. Mucus is the gooey stuff that runs from your nose when you've got a cold. Actually, it is always present in your nose, whether you are sick or well. Snot is your friend!

LESTER'S TOP TEN COLLOQUIA... WHATEVERS FOR MUCUS

1. Snot
2. "Your friend"
3. Phlegm Cakes
4. Schnotskis
5. Shooters
6. Boogers
7. Green Hornets
8. Loogies
9. Oysters
10. Nose Jam

protects your body from having to deal with even more gunk coming in. When you blow your nose or clear your throat, out comes snot...and with it comes the dirt and germs that you breathed in.

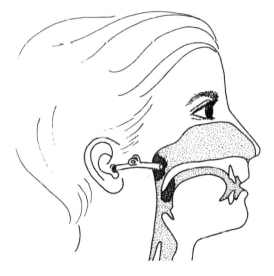

Here's a picture of the NASAL PASSAGE, where you'll find the mucus factory. Snot is like sticky glue. It traps the dirt and germs floating in the air that get into your nose and throat. If you are fighting off a cold, snot

I know that some of you out there find the subject of snot a tad bit disturbing, a little shocking, maybe even disgustingly gross. But the point of this book is to answer the questions you ask. That's what I'm here for...to find out things you want to know, that you need to know. I'm your personal scientist. I'm Beakman. And if I have to go up a nose, then up a nose I will go!

Boring's Definitions

Prof. I. M. Boring
Inert State University

Hello, it is I again, Professor I.M. Boring. While the cast of "Beakman's World" was off researching new ways to present science to the world, I managed to infiltrate the pages of this text and add my own section. What follows are nice, precise, concise...okay, boring...definitions of some of the terms you will find in this book.

AIR PRESSURE: The force per unit area that the air exerts on any surface in contact with it.

ALTERNATING CURRENT (A.C.): A form of electric current that changes direction periodically.

ARTERIES: Vascular tubes that carry blood from the heart.

CAPILLARIES: Minute blood vessels that connect arteries and veins.

CELLS: Microscopic functional and structural units of all living organisms, consisting of a nucleus, cytoplasm, and a living membrane.

CELLULOSE: A polymer found in plant tissues and fibers that is used in the manufacturing of paper.

CHLOROPHYLL: Any of several green plant pigments which function as photoreceptors of light energy for photosynthesis.

CIRCUIT: A closed path through which an electric current may flow.

COMBUSTION: The stroke in an engine when expanding gases apply pressure to the piston.

COMPRESSION: The stroke in an engine when the piston moves up and combines the gasoline and the air.

CONDENSATION: The process by which water vapor becomes a liquid.

CONTRACTION: The action or process of becoming smaller or pressed together (e.g. a gas upon cooling).

CRUST: The outermost solid layer of the earth, mostly consisting of crystalling rock.

DIRECT CURRENT (D.C.): Electric current that flows only in one direction.

ERUPTION: The ejection of solid, liquid, or gaseous material from a volcano.

EVAPORATION: The conversion of a liquid to a vaporous state by the addition of latent heat.

EXPANSION: Process in which the constant mass of a substance increases.

FILAMENT: Metallic wire or ribbon in a light bulb which heats up and produces light when an electric current passes through it.

GRAVITY: The attractive central gravitational force exerted by a celestial body, such as the earth.

INERTIA: The property of matter which manifests itself as a resistance to any change in the momentum of a body.

INTAKE: The stroke of an engine when fluid is admitted to the cylinder.

LAVA: Molten extrusive material that reaches the earth's surface through volcanic vents and fissures.

MAGMA: Molten matter beneath the earth's crust that often cools and and hardens to form igneous rock.

MANTLE: The intermediate small zone of the earth below the crust and above the core.

MASS: A quantitative measure of a body's resistance to acceleration.

MOLECULES: A group of atoms held together by chemical forces. A molecule is the smallest unit of matter which can exist by itself and retain all its chemical properties.

MUCUS: A viscous liquid secreted by the mucous glands as a protectant.

RESISTANCE: The opposition a material or a device offers to the flow of electricity.

SURFACE TENSION: The force acting on the surface of a liquid, tending to minimize the area of the surface.

VEINS: Thin-walled blood vessels that carry blood from the capillaries to the heart.

WATER CYCLE: The complete cycle through which water passes, from oceans through the atmosphere, to land, and then back to the oceans.

WATER VAPOR: Water in the form of a vapor, especially when below the boiling point and diffused.

BEAKMANIA

"Hey, wake up! It's time to expand your intellect! Here he is, the Caesar of science...the Pharoah of facts...the Archduke of the arcane...the one...the only...the Beakman!"

Q: How many cookies will the average American eat in a lifetime?

A: Over 35,000 cookies.

Q: Hey, Beakman, are there any prehistoric animals still left on Earth?

A: There's the crocodile, sharks, cockroaches of course, Australia's duck-billed platypus, the turtle, and a fish called the coelacanth, which lives off the coast of Southern Africa, and is four hundred million years old!

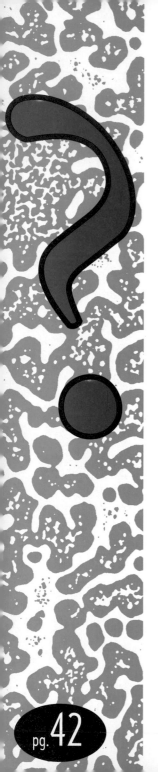

Q: What's the most commonly used word in the English language?

A: "Ketchup"...just kidding. It's actually a tiny, one-letter word..."I."

Q: Beakman, how much do the average pair of feet sweat in a day?

A: Try one cup. On second thought, don't try it.

Q: How fast does air come out of your nostrils?

A: Air can pass through your nostrils at speeds of up to 100 miles per hour. It's like having a small hurricane in your head! By the way, each day, your nose exhales enough air to fill 1,800 basketballs.

Q: Okay, wiseguy, who's buried in Grant's Tomb?

A: Ulysses S. Grant...and his wife, Julia.

Blood, Beakmania & Dreams

"I had a dream about this show last night."

"I had a dream about sardines...millions of 'em."

Chapter

FACT!

The human body produces more than 25,000 quarts of saliva in its lifetime. That's more than enough to fill two swimming pools with spit.

pg. 46

Blood

"How much blood is in the human body?"

The average person has about five liters (or ten-and-a-half pints) of blood in their body.

The heart pumps this blood throughout the body in tubes called VEINS, ARTERIES, and CAPILLARIES. If you laid all these tubes end-to-end, they'd reach around the world two-and-a-half times!

"Why do we have blood?" Because blood has work to do! Blood has three full-time jobs, not counting the part-time job at the video store.

BLOOD'S THREE FULL-TIME JOBS:

1. Deliver food and oxygen to the billions of cells in your body.

2. Remove the cells' waste products and take them to the kidneys and lungs. The kidneys filter out the waste products, and the lungs expel carbon dioxide into the air.

3. Protect the body against germs.

Dreams

"What are dreams?"

Dreams come from your imagination. Let me put it this way. Life is like shopping. When you go shopping, you're collecting things. You go through life collecting things, too. Instead of bread, milk, and jawbreakers, the things you collect in life are:

Information
Experiences
Memories
Visual images of stuff

These things stay in your mind.

"Well, how does this make dreams?"

Everyone has something called their **CONSCIOUS MIND** and their **UNCONSCIOUS MIND**. It's the way these two things work together which gives each of us our own individual imagination!

THE CONSCIOUS MIND is all the things that you are aware of, like:

What time it is.
What you're thinking.
What you're doing.
And the fly that's buzzing around your head.

Your conscious mind processes all these experiences and information and stores them in your memory.

THE UNCONSCIOUS MIND, however, is a little trickier. It's not limited to reality, and is more playful. When the conscious mind goes to sleep...that's when the unconscious mind comes out to party! The unconscious mind is the writer of our dreams.

If you see a palm tree, the conscious mind says, "That's a palm tree." And the unconscious mind imagines: "Hawaii, pink flamingos, warm weather, the time Gilligan got hit on the head with a coconut."

If you see a lobster, the conscious mind says, "That's a lobster." And the unconscious mind imagines: "The ocean, Maine, melted butter, grown-ups with bibs on."

So, a dream could take you from a lobster to...melted butter to...your family refrigerator to...the milk in your refrigerator to...a cow to..."Old McDonald Had A Farm" to...the farm your Grandpa grew up on to...Christmas at your grandparents to...the new bike you got as a present.

Our imagination can give us scary, as well as pleasant dreams. They can seem so real. Sometimes you can actually choose what you dream about. Right before you go to sleep, think about someone or something you want to dream about. Think about everything that a person or thing means to you. If it doesn't work the first time, don't give up. It will work eventually. And when it does, it's outstanding!

The **BEAKMAN CHALLENGE**

"I challenge you to jam a toilet plunger handle through a piece of tissue paper."

You're gonna need:

- a sheet of tissue paper
- a paper towel tube
- a rubber band
- a toilet plunger
  (or a broom handle)
- one to two cups of salt

Warning

"Experiments should be performed at home only with adult supervision and all appropriate safety precautions should be followed exactly and no substitutions should be used."

Here we go! Okay, take your paper towel tube and, using the rubber band, attach the tissue around the end of the tube. Then pour salt into the bottom of the tube to a depth of at least six inches.

Now take your plunger--not the business end, please--and try to jam it through the tissue. Be sure to hold the tube, not the tissue, just above the rubber band. It's not that easy is it? In fact, it's darn near impossible, and you want to know why?

You see, there are lots and lots of tiny air spaces between the grains of salt. When the plunger strikes--and, by the way, that would be a great title for a movie--the energy from the blow goes into pushing the salt crystals closer together and against the sides of the tube. This takes up the entire force of the blow. There's no energy left to tear the tissue paper!

BEAKMANIA

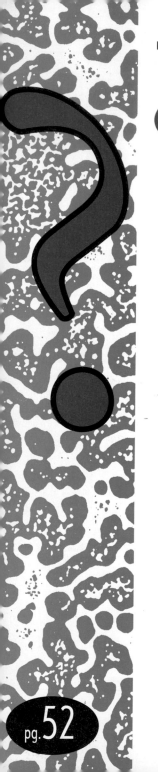

"Are you ready? It's time to inundate your intellect! Here he is...the umpire of understanding...the dean of discovery...the maitre d' of memory...the one...the only...the Beakman!"

Q: How many words are there in the English language?

A: There are over 400,000. Interestingly enough, the average person uses only 3,000.

Q: Dear Beakman, how fast can the fastest dog run?

A: The greyhound, which is the fastest dog, can reach speeds of up to 41.7 miles per hour.

Q: What's the longest word in the English language?

A: Well, there's lots of scientific words that go on forever...but for your regular day-to-day usage, try...floccinaucinihilipilification. It means "the act of judging a bit of information to be utterly worthless."

floccinaucinihilipilification

Q: How many bones are there in the human body?

A: 206.

Q: How old is the sun?

A: Astronomers estimate that the sun is about four-and-a-half billion years old.

Q: How powerful is a lightning storm?

A: One lightning bolt can contain enough electricity to light 200,000 homes. By the way, one good thing about lightning storms is that they break loose the nitrogen in the air, which falls to the ground and then acts as a natural fertilizing agent for plants, trees, crops, and your front lawn.

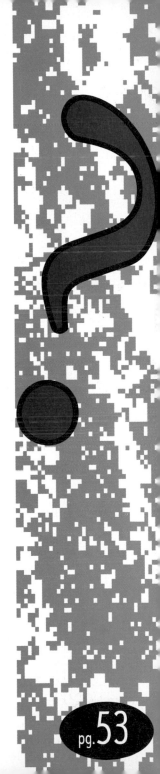

Leaves, Beakmania & Paper

"Hey, leave me that paper!"

"No way, I've got to write a paper about leaves."

Chapter

FACT!

The length of the wings of a jumbo jet is 196 feet. That's longer than the Wright Brothers' first flight.

Leaves

"Why do leaves change color?"

Technically, leaves don't change color--they <u>turn</u> color. I know that sounds confusing, but what really happens is that they lose one color...green.

Take a maple leaf, for example. It has lots of colors...red, yellow, orange. But the one we see the most is green. That's because the leaf is mostly full of a green chemical called **CHLOROPHYLL**. In the fall, the leaf runs out of chlorophyll. The green color goes away, and we see the other colors that were there the whole time.

"What's the chlorophyll doing in the leaf in the first place?"

An excellent question. See, chlorophyll helps produce food for the tree. Water and carbon dioxide mix together with the help of the chlorophyll and the energy of sunlight, in what's called **PHOTOSYNTHESIS**. "Photo" from the Greek word for light...as in sunlight, and "synthesis" which means to make stuff. In addition to helping make food for the tree, leaves give off the oxygen we need to live. And when we breathe out, we breathe out the carbon dioxide the tree needs to live.

Paper

"How do you recycle paper?"

Aha! A question for the nineties and beyond! If you don't know what recycling is, it's using something more than once intsead of throwing it away.

Now, paper is made from something called CELLULOSE. We get cellulose from cutting down and grinding up trees. So when you recycle paper, in many ways you are saving trees.

When you're done with your newspaper and you take it to a recycling center or leave it outside your house to be picked up, it's shipped off to a paper mill to be recycled.

You can make your own recycled paper by following the easy directions on the next page.

"Experiments should be performed at home only with adult supervision and all appropriate safety precautions should be followed exactly and no substitutions should be used."

You'll need: 1 -- A newspaper. 2 -- A coat hanger. 3 -- A pair of pantyhose. 4 -- A food processor. 5 -- White glue. 6 -- Sink and water. 7 -- Permission from your family.

Let's do it!

1. Tear two full pages of newspaper into strips and then tear those strips into tiny squares. Put the pieces into the food processor and add enough water to cover them. You can also add some good old dryer lint for texture. Now you need a grown-up person to turn the machine on. Run the food processor for about three minutes -- until the paper disappears into a disgusting gray gunk.

2. Undo the coat hanger and bend it into a square, carefully, please! Stretch the pantyhose over the wire square and tie knots in the ends. Clip off the rest of the pantyhose.

3. To the sink -- put a stopper in the drain and dump the gray gunk in. Add four or five inches of water and two spoonfuls of white glue into the mix and stir it all up with your hands. Get your pantyhose square and submerge it in the gunk until it's on the bottom of the sink. Lift the square out slowly -- counting to twenty while you lift will help. When you get the square to the top, let the water drip off for a whole minute -- count slowly to sixty.

4. Hang the square to dry. It's best to hang it outside in the sunshine, but if you can't, hang it somewhere where it won't be disturbed. It's very important that you let the gunk completely dry, or your recycled paper will be wrecked. Be patient!

5. When the paper is dry, carefully peel it from the screen, and use it just like real paper. Hey, it is real paper! In fact, it's better! It's recycled paper! In fact, this is recycled paper; yes, this book is printed on recycled paper!

Famous Person

Name: Galileo Galilei
Born: 1564
Died: 1642

Claim to fame: Made several significant contributions to modern scientific thought, including discovering the law of falling bodies and re-establishing mathematics as the basis for solving scientific problems. Oh, and he also improved a little thing called the telescope.

Famous quote: "The Book of Nature...is written in mathematical characters."

Favorite soccer team: AC Milan.

Until the end of the 1500s, people believed that if you dropped two objects of different mass to the ground from the same height at the same time, the heavier of the two would hit the ground first. Galileo disagreed with this and by experimenting, he was able to prove himself correct. According to legend he dropped two cannon balls (one large, one small) from the Leaning Tower of Pisa. They struck the ground at nearly the same time. Galileo concluded that the only difference was caused by the resistance of the air upon the cannon balls.

If Galileo were in a televison studio today, he might try the same experiment with an eggplant and a piece of paper.

Now, if it's a flat piece of paper, the eggplant will easily hit first. Why? It's that air resistance thing again. But if you crumple the paper up into a ball and drop the two objects again...see, they land at approximately the same time.

AMAZING UNITS OF MEASURE

Don't be a pig...share these with your friends.

"Hey, I resent that... I'm a hog, not a pig."

Chain: A unit of length equal to either 66 feet (called a "surveyor's chain") or 100 feet (called an "engineer's chain).

Dram: Unit of apothecaries' weight, equal to 60 grains or 1/8 ounce.

Farad: Unit of capacitance equal to one coulomb per volt.

Fathom: A unit of length (usually used in nautical measurement) equal to six feet.

Furlong: Unit of distance equal to 220 yards or 1/8 mile.

Hectare: A metric unit of surface or land, equal to 10,000 square meters (about 2.471 acres).

Hogshead: Unit of liquid measure, usually equal to 63 gallons of wine.

League: Unit of distance, usually estimated at around three miles.

Peck: A dry measure of 8 quarts; the fourth part of a bushel, equal to 537.6 cubic inches.

Quintal: A unit of metric weight equal to 100 kilograms or 220.462 pounds.

Stone: A British unit of weight equal to 14 pounds.

Tesla: A unit of magnetic induction equal to one weber per square meter.

BEAKMANIA

"Prepare yourselves! It's time to nudge your noggin! Here he is, the duke of data...the squire of scholarship...the emir of the enigmatic...the one...the only...the Beakman!"

Q: What country has the most coastline?

A: If you count all the islands, the answer is...Canada.

Q: Yo, Beakman. What's the longest snake in the world?

A: The anaconda--it can measure up to 30 feet!

Q: How much is a "cord" of wood?

A: A cord of wood measures 4 feet by 4 feet by 8 feet. By the way, a cord of wood can produce about 250 Sunday newspapers.

Q: Those are good answers, but how about some cool animal facts.

A: Okay, how about this...there are about 1 million alligators in the U.S., and not one of them can walk backwards...the Texas horned toad can squirt blood from the corner of its eyes...a bootlace worm can grow up to 250 feet long.

Q: Hey, Beakman, besides Milton Berle, what are some of the oldest living things on Earth?

A: There's a bristlecone pine tree in Northern California which is already 4,600 years old and a lichen from Antarctica that is thought to be 10,000 years old!

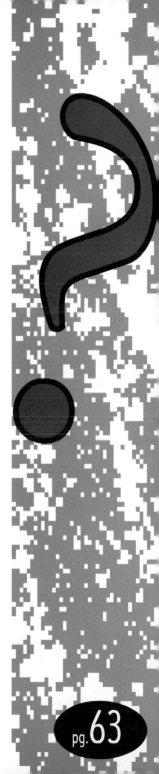

Soap, Beakmania & Auto Engines

"I can't wait to learn about auto engines; I haven't been able to start my car in weeks."

"Maybe the engine's cold."

Chapter

FACT!

A flamingo can only eat when its head is upside down because that's how it strains the water out of its food.

pg. 66

Soap

"How does soap work?"

Take the plastic strawberry basket and place it on top of the water...see it floats on top of the water's skin. Now spray the water with soap...the basket sinks because the soap breaks down the surface tension!

Soap is a very interesting thing. It actually works by making water wetter (try saying that three times fast). How do you make water wetter? See, water has a kind of a skin, which we call SURFACE TENSION. Soap weakens the surface tension.

Test this out for yourself. You'll need: 1. A plastic strawberry basket. 2. A bucket of water. 3. A spray bottle full of soap and water.

"But how does breaking down the surface tension get stuff clean?"

Good question. See, surface tension prevents the water from getting to the pieces of dirt between the fibers of your clothing. But soap, plus a little elbow grease (you know, rubbing) makes the water wetter, so it can get to all the nooks and crannies of your clothing.

Auto Engines

"How does gas make a car go?"

Simple Answer:
It explodes! Gasoline, believe it or not has the same explosive power as dynamite!

Not-So-Simple Answer:
To really understand this, we'll have to get inside an engine and see how the pistons and the valves and the crankshaft work.

The piston works in four steps, called STROKES.

The first stroke is called INTAKE. The intake valve opens and the piston moves down. Gasoline and air are drawn into the cylinder.

The second stroke is called COMPRESSION. In compression, the intake valve closes and the piston moves up, compressing the gasoline and the air.

The third stroke is COMBUSTION or THE POWER STROKE. Here, both the intake and the exhaust valves are closed...the spark plug sparks...the gasoline vapor explodes, and the piston is slammed down!

Now comes the fourth stroke, called EXHAUST. The exhaust valve opens and the piston moves up, pushing the smoke from the explosion out into the air.

This cycle happens over and over again at a very high rate of speed.

BEAKMAN CHALLENGE

"I challenge you to make a can come back to you when you call it."

You're gonna need:

- a coffee can
- two plastic tops
- a rubber band
- two small sticks
- a pair of scissors
- a piece of tape
- and a weight

Warning

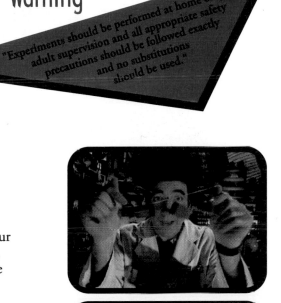

"Experiments should be performed at home only with adult supervision and all appropriate safety precautions should be followed exactly and no substitutions should be used."

Use a can opener to take both ends off your coffee can. You take your two plastic lids, and use your scissors to punch a little hole through the center of each of them.

Put the rubber band through the hole in one of the lids. Now attach it to the lid with the stick. You tape the weight to one of the strands of the rubber band. Try and get it in the middle there. Okay, put the lid on the can and pull the rubber band through the can.

Attach the rubber band to the other lid with a stick the way you attached it to the first one.

Then give your can a name...roll it away from you...and right before your eyes...your can comes back to you!

See, when you roll the can away, the rubber band twists around itself. Twisting a rubber band stores up energy in it. When the rubber band gets fully twisted, the can stops moving. Since ENERGY HAS TO GO SOMEWHERE, the energy in the rubber band has to go somewhere. It goes into untwisting itself, and that starts the can rolling back to you!

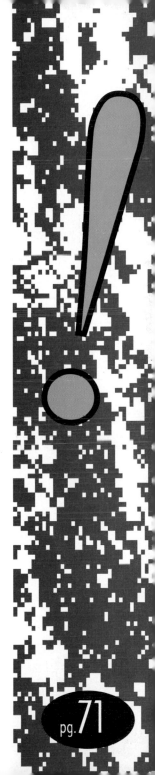

BEAKMANIA

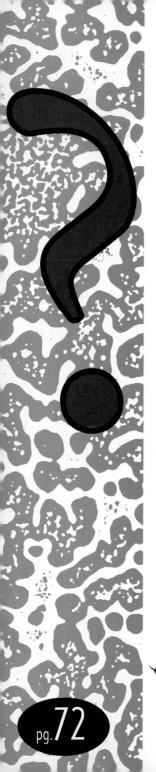

"Get ready! It's time to broaden your brain! Here he is...the colossus of clarity...the tribune of trivia...the hep cat of what's that...the one...the only...the Beakman!"

Q: Why are car tires black? I think pink tires would look really cool.

A: Tires are black because a black substance called carbon is added. If your tires were made without carbon, they'd erase themselves in a few miles, like your pink pencil eraser.

Q: What was the heaviest animal ever?

A: Many people would guess that it's one of the dinosaurs, but in fact, it's the blue whale. It can weigh more than 16 elephants (or more than 1,600 human beings) -- more than 200 tons!

Q: Dear Beakman, do birds sweat?

A: Only jailbirds.

Q: Hey, Beakdude, do aircraft carriers get good gas mileage?

A: It's Beakman, dude. And no, they don't. How does six inches per gallon sound? On the other hand, a Monarch butterfly can go 620 miles without fueling up on food.

Q: What's the capital of South Dakota?

A: Pierre. And that's pronounced "Peer," not "Pierre," like a French guy's name.

Q: Beakman, I really like those cool animal facts. Got any more?

A: Sure...woodpeckers use their beaks as icepicks in the winter...all primates (monkeys, gorillas, orangutans, humans) have fingerprints...penguins are near-sighted.

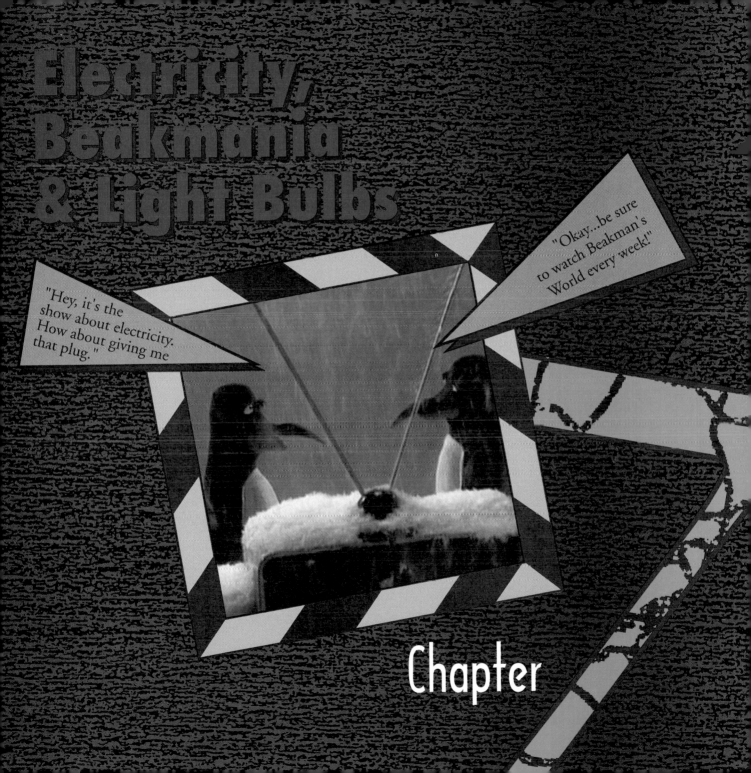

FACT!

Most bears use their left paws more than their right.

pg. 76

Electricity

"What is electricity?"

Electricity is simply the flow of electrical energy through an unbroken path. The name of that path is a CIRCUIT.

"Why do electrical plugs have two prongs?"

Although some actually have three, at least two prongs are necessary because electricity flows in a loop. It takes two prongs to make a loop.

A loop makes the stuff plugs are attached to work.

"Why doesn't electricity just flow out of a plug all over the floor?"

Because electricity really isn't a thing. You can't hold it in your hand or keep it in a jar. Electricity is an event. It's when something happens, like a basketball game.

The Two Types Of Electricity

AC (Alternating Current): This is the kind of electricity we get from plugs, and use for our household appliances. It changes its direction (alternates) many times a second.

DC (Direct Current): This is the kind of electricity we get from batteries. It flows in one direction.

AC/DC: This is a heavy metal band.

Light Bulbs

"How does a lightbulb work?"

In general, electrons flow smoothly until their path narrows. Then they start rubbing and bumping up against each other, trying to go forward. When the path narrows, that's called RESISTANCE. A light bulb resists the flow of electrons, and that makes it heat up and start to glow. And that's why it gets bright.

When you turn on the light bulb, the electricity flows freely until it gets to the thin wire called the FILAMENT.

You might be wondering why the filament glows and the other wires don't. It's very simple. See, the other wires are thicker, so they have less resistance and don't heat up.

It's amazing when you think about how much has changed since the invention of the light bulb. Just think about this--in the old days, when someone had a good idea, a candle appeared over their head!

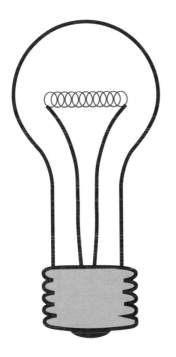

That's where the resistance comes in. The filament heats up to 4,500 degrees Fahrenheit. That makes the filament glow white hot, and that's how it lights up your life.

Famous Person

Name: Thomas Alva Edison
Born: 1847
Died: 1931

Claim to fame: Possibly the world's greatest inventor. Patented more than 1,000 inventions in his lifetime, including the light bulb and the phonograph.

Famous quote: "Genius is 1% inspiration and 99% perspiration." (does not apply to birds)

Biggest gripe: His middle name.

WHICH OF THESE THINGS DID EDISON INVENT OR IMPROVE UPON?

A) Electric Vote-Recording Machine
B) Phonograph (Record Player)
C) Electric Light Bulb
D) Stock Ticker
E) Typewriter
F) Telephone
G) Motion Picture Camera
H) Storage Battery
I) Cement Mixer
J) Dictaphone
K) Duplicating Machine
L) The Juiceman® Electric Juicer

Answer: All, except for L.

BEAKMAN'S TOP TEN ELEMENTS

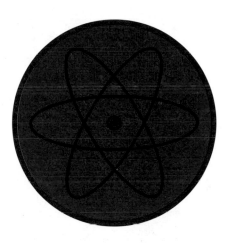

10. **Oxygen (O):** Hey, if we didn't include this one, we wouldn't be alive!

9. **Helium (He):** It makes balloons and blimps float through the air.

8. **Tungsten (W):** This is what light bulb filaments are made of.

7. **Sodium (Na):** You're probably very familiar with this element, since it's in salt. Think about that the next time you eat french fries.

6. **Aluminum (Al):** Come on! Everything from baseball bats to foil to siding for your house.

5. **Carbon (C):** A very important element. Not only is it used in tires and pencils, but it helps us learn about past civilization by seeing how old things are (through a process called "Carbon Dating").

4. **Beakmanium (Bk):** Okay, just kidding about this one. But wouldn't it be great to have an element named after you? There are a bunch of them already, like Einsteinium and Lawrencium.

3. **Californium (Cf):** With a name like this, you'd think it would be an incredibly mellow, laid-back element, but it's actually very dangerous and radioactive.

2. **Molybdenum (Mo):** This is an element used to make tools; but I just like the word.

1. **Mercury (Hg):** Not only is it used in barometers and thermometers, but if you've ever seen it poured out on a table, it's just incredibly amazing.

BEAKMANIA

"Attention! It's time to gear up your grey matter! Here he is, the constable of cognizance...the pasha of perception...the Bob Hope of the straight dope...the one...the only...the Beakman!"

Q: Beeeeekman, how many beeeekeeeepers are there in the United States?

A: None of your beeswax...okay, okay, maybeeee...211,000.

Q: Hey Beakman, how many shots can a skunk get off before it has to reload?

A: I suppose this question means how much of that smelly stuff can a skunk squirt before it has to store up again for its next shot? Answer: Enough for six squirts.

Q: Beakman, what's the world's record for walking on your hands?

A: I don't let anyone walk on my hands. But Johan Hurlinger of Austria walked 871 miles on his hands.

Q: Here's one for you. Are carrots really good for your eyes?

A: Yeah, but they look really silly on the bridge of your nose. Actually, carrots are full of Vitamin A, which is very good for people who have trouble seeing at night.

Q: Why are yawns contagious?

A: (Yawn) Huh? Oh. No one knows.

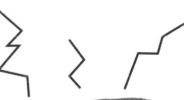

Q: Are electric eels really electric?

A: You betcha. In fact, a shock from an electric eel can measure up to 650 volts...enough to throw a person (your favorite uncle) across a room.

FACT!

The American Bald Eagle builds a nest which can weigh four thousand pounds. That's as much as a Dodge Dart!

pg. 86

Sound

"What is sound?"

This is an oscilloscope. It's a fancy name for a machine that lets you see patterns of sound. To make your own Beakman Home Oscilloscope, check out pages 90 and 91.

Sound is stuff vibrating. When we talk, or clap our hands or an alarm goes off, it creates vibrations in the air around us. And those vibrations travel at about 780 miles per hour. Those vibrations, in turn, vibrate in your ear which is how you hear sound.

THINGS SOUND CAN TRAVEL THROUGH

1. Air
2. Water
3. Wood
4. Cheese
5. String

Try making sound travel on a string.

Put a hole in the end of each can, place a string through them, and tie knots inside each can. Pull the string tight and you're ready to play Alexander Graham Bell, the inventor of the telephone. Talk into one can and

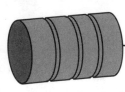 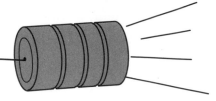

somebody listening on the other can can hear you.

See, your voice makes the air in the can vibrate...which makes the end of the can vibrate...which makes the string vibrate...which makes the end of the other can vibrate...which makes the air in the other can vibrate. That air penetrates your ear, which sends signals to your brain where you hear them.

Explosions

"What is an explosion, and can you blow some stuff up?"

An explosion is when stuff gets really big, really fast. And it's not just things like bombs and fires.

Take popcorn. Pay for it first, of course. You see, inside a kernel of popcorn is a little bit of water. When you heat that water, it becomes steam and expands.

That steam's gotta burst out of there, so it turns into a big, fluffy piece of popcorn.

"Let's try another one."

Warning: Don't put your face over it. Then, when you're ready...and all precautions have been taken...drop the fizzy tablet into the film thingy, put the cap on, and run!

Experiments should be performed at home only with adult supervision. You can never be too careful when you're messing around with explosive substances.

You're gonna need three things...a little plastic film can thingy...water...and a fizzy antacid tablet. Put some water into the film can thingy.

Isn't that cool? When the tablet hits the water, carbon dioxide is produced real fast and it needs to get out. The fastest way out is to blow the cap off.

Construction companies use carefully controlled explosions to destroy old and sometimes unsafe structures.

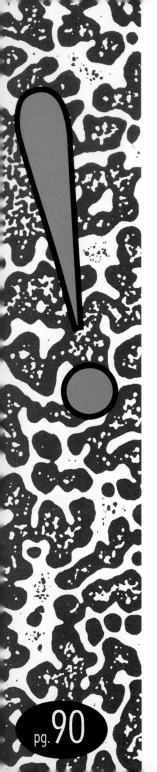

The BEAKMAN CHALLENGE

"I challenge you to see the vibrations your voice makes."

You're gonna need:

- a cut-up balloon
- a rubber band
- some glue
- a tiny, tiny mirror
- a flashlight
- a piece of card or posterboard
- and a can.

Warning

"Experiments should be performed at home only with adult supervision and all appropriate safety precautions should be followed exactly and no substitutions should be used."

Carefully use a can opener to open both ends of the can. Then you take your cut-up balloon, stretch it tightly over one end and secure it with a rubber band. When I talk into the can...the sound of my voice vibrates the balloon.

Don't put the mirror right in the middle. It won't work as well.

Now, let's really see the sound! Put a little glue on the back of the mirror, and stick the mirror on the balloon near the edge.

Set the card up against something. Then shine the flashlight so it reflects off the mirror and onto the card. Now speak into the can. The reflection should vibrate as you speak. Try making different sounds and noises...see how the reflection changes. Congratulations. You've just "seen" sound!

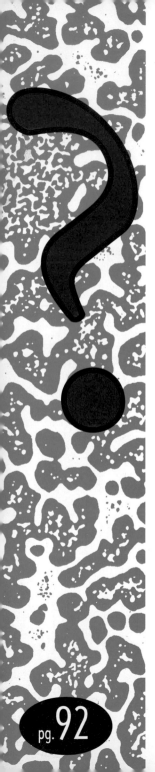

BEAKMANIA

"Get ready to crank up your cranium! Here he is, the commander of comprehension...the deacon of dissemination...the Charlemagne of shenanigans...the one...the only...the Beakman!"

Q: Hey, Beakman, how long did the average Caveman live?

A: The average caveman lived 18 years. That means he had a mid-life crisis at age 9.

Q: Yo, Beakman, what's the deal with barber poles?

A: Barber poles date from medieval times, when barbers were surgeons; the red and white pole was a symbol of blood and bandages.

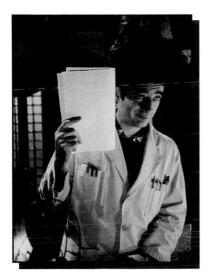

Q: I say a man's hair grows much faster than a woman's. My friend says a woman's does. Who pays for lunch?

A: You do. A woman's hair grows faster than a man's.

Q: Who won the 1969 World Series?

A: The Mets, of course.

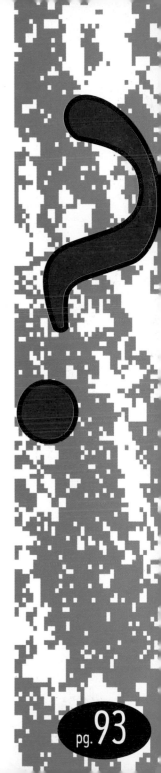

Q: Are snakes the only animals that shed their skin?

A: Not at all. In fact, we humans shed our skin too--to the tune of about 40 pounds per year!

Q: How long does it take light to get from the Sun to the Earth?

A: Assuming the trip is non-stop, 8 minutes. But it takes another week to find its luggage.

"If you have a question about how the world works, go to the library and look it up...or ask your favorite teacher, or your friends or family, or write us at:"

Beakman's World
P.O. Box 30087
Kansas City, MO 64112

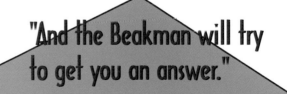

"And the Beakman will try to get you an answer."

Well, that's about all the room we have left for now. Remember to keep watching "Beakman's World" on your local TV station.

Before we leave, we want you to try one more thing. First, grab a sheet of paper...any sheet of paper. Now...try to fold your sheet of paper more than nine times.

Pretty tough, isn't it? In fact, it's impossible. See, if you keep doubling the thickness of something, pretty soon it's thicker than it is wide and you can't fold it anymore. By the time you try folding the paper for the tenth time, you are attempting to fold more than 500 layers (or one REAM) of paper. It's all about geometry...it's all about science...it's all about fun!

pg. 96

And we're all out of time! See you next time on "Beakman's World!"